SCIENCE FILES
GLASS

SCIENCE FILES – GLASS
was produced by

David West 👫 Children's Books
7 Princeton Court
55 Felsham Road
London SW15 1AZ

Designers: Rob Shone, Fiona Thorne, David West
Editor: James Pickering
Picture Research: Carrie Haines

First published in Great Britain in 2001 by
Heinemann Library, Halley Court, Jordan Hill,
Oxford OX2 8EJ, a division of Reed Educational and
Professional Publishing Limited.

OXFORD MELBOURNE AUCKLAND
JOHANNESBURG BLANTYRE GABORONE
IBADAN PORTSMOUTH (NH) USA CHICAGO

05 04 03 02 01
10 9 8 7 6 5 4 3 2 1

ISBN 0 431 14303 X (HB)
ISBN 0 431 14309 9 (PB)

British Library Cataloguing in Publication Data

Parker, Steve, 1952 -
Glass. - (Science files)
1. Glass
I. Title
620.1'44

Printed and bound in Spain by Bookprint, S.L., Barcelona

PHOTO CREDITS :
Abbreviations: t-top, m-middle, b-bottom, r-right,
l-left.

Front cover - bl & 28/29 (Bildagentur
Schuster/Bramaz), tr & 8 - Robert Harding Picture
Library. m & 17b (Eileen Tweedy) - The Art Archive.
br & 11m - Ann Ronan Picture Library. 3 & 19b
(Lee Frost), 7b, 22t (Martyn F. Chillmaid), 11t (Adam
Woolfitt), 16b (M.H. Black), 20t (Raj Kamal), 25br
(Esben Hardt), 27b (Hartmann/Sachs/Phototake,
NYC), 12t, 14l & r, 16mr, 23t, 25l - Robert Harding
Picture Library. 4t, 13m (Victor de Schwanberg), 5b
(Philippe Plailly), 6l (Tony Craddock), 10mr, 11mr
(Rosenfeld Images Ltd), 13tl (Frank Morgan), 20m
(Mehau Kulyk), 21t, 22b (Geoff Tompkinson), 26t,
26/27t (David Parker), 26b (Ed Young), 29t
(Maximilian Stock Ltd), 29b - Science Photo Library.
4/5, 16t Waltraud Krase/D.G. Bank, Berlin. 5t, 10ml -
Ann Ronan Picture Library. 14m, 24t - Glass
Manufacturing Federation. 7br (Museo Civico
Udine/Dagli Orti), 9tl (Eileen Tweedy) - The Art
Archive. 23m (Paul Keevil), 15b, 28bl & br - Mary
Evans Picture Library. 8b, 13br - Spectrum Colour
Library. 14/15b - Glassworks, Hampton.

Every effort has been made to trace the copyright
holders and we apologise in advance for any
unintentional omissions. We would be pleased to
insert the appropriate acknowledgement in any
subsequent edition of this publication.

*An explanation of difficult words can be
found in the glossary on page 30.*

SCIENCE FILES

GLASS

Steve Parker

Heinemann
LIBRARY

CONTENTS

Factories make millions of glass bottles every day. These are some of the easiest types of glass products to recycle.

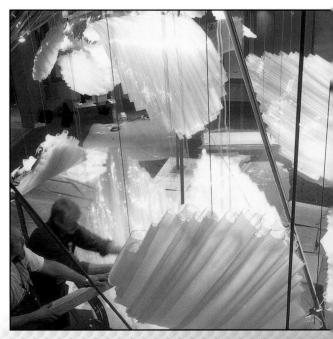

INTRODUCTION

One of the world's most important inventions is something that we hardly see. It is specially designed to be invisible. Glass protects our homes from the wind, rain and cold, and lets us see our drinks in their containers. Glass is hardly ever noticed, but it's all around us. We use it every day, and it's an easy substance to recycle. Glass is very hi-tech, too. Special types of glass are used in computers, lasers, spectacles, cameras, electronic machines, light bulbs and bright, sparkling decorations. A world without glass would be dark and dull!

This engraving shows glass-making, one of the oldest crafts. Skilled people have shaped and coloured glass by hand for thousands of years. The raw materials for glass are mainly sand and limestone.

Glass is beautiful. Amazing glass 'clouds' are suspended in the hall of DG Bank, Berlin.

Incredibly thin, long, bendy rods of glass carry flashes of laser light, in fibre-optic telephone cables.

Glass is very difficult to describe. One technical name for it is a 'supercooled liquid'. This means glass is a clear, colourless liquid, like water. It has cooled down to normal temperature after being made, and become hard and stiff. It's still just about a liquid, rather than a solid, but it can hardly run or flow any more.

This glass building is at Futuroscope, Poitiers, France. Its shape is based on the shapes of crystals in sand – the main mineral used in glass.

LIQUID OR SOLID?

Another technical name for glass is an 'amorphous solid'. (*Amorphous* means 'no shape'.) Under a microscope, most solid substances are made up of tiny parts such as crystals or molecules. Glass is not. It has no particular tiny shapes or structures inside.

MAKING GLASS

The most important raw material for making glass is sand. This is the mineral silica, which contains the chemicals silicon and oxygen, as silicon dioxide (SiO_2). Silica is heated with other minerals, such as limestone (calcium carbonate) and soda ash (sodium carbonate). The mixture melts and is then cooled quickly to form glass.

Sand (top) and limestone (above) are important raw materials for most types of glass. They are dug from huge quarries and stored ready for use.

Facts from the **PAST**

About 6,000 years ago glass was used as a hard, shiny covering, or glaze, on beads. Early glass jars and bowls were made in moulds about 3,500 years ago. The next stage, glass-blowing, began some 2,100 years ago.

A 2,000-year-old glass flask.

GLASS-BLOWING

When air blows into a liquid, it forms a bubble. Glass heated to more than about 1,000°C becomes a liquid – molten glass. Blow through a long pipe into it and a bubble forms inside. Using a lot of skill, the result can be a beautiful piece of glassware such as a goblet, vase or cup.

AGE-OLD CRAFT

The craft of glass-blowing has changed very little for almost 2,000 years. A long metal tube, the blow-pipe, is dipped into a container of very hot, melted glass. The blow-pipe is twirled around to collect a blob of glass on its end – like gathering syrup with a spoon.

The glass-blower may reheat the glass (right), to keep it soft while it is blown and shaped, into items such as wine glasses (left).

The ship in this 19th century blown-glass bottle was inserted with its masts flat. The masts were pulled upright with a thread.

BLOWING A BUBBLE

The glass-blower puffs down the blow-pipe to push air into the blob of molten glass, which expands like a balloon. Twisting the blow-pipe keeps the growing 'bubble' of glass, called the *parison*, smooth and round. The glass-blower may hold it against various surfaces, or place it in a hollow mould. Gradually the glass is blown, twisted and pressed. It cools and hardens into its final shape.

Ideas for the FUTURE

Imagine a glass bubble so big that it covered a city! But this could not happen here on Earth. Our planet's gravity gives glass weight, which would make a giant glass bubble sag and crack. However, in space there is no gravity. Glass could be blown into a huge dome, which might then be used to cover a Moon base.

Glass – keeps air in and space out?

TOOLS AND TECHNIQUES

Each stage of glass-blowing has its special tools and techniques. The blob of molten glass collected on the end of the blow-pipe is called the *gather*. This is rolled on a smooth metal slab, a method known as *marvering*, to make a longer shape called the parison.

The glass-blower keeps the bubble of glass rolling or twirling to make sure it stays smooth and round. Extra pieces of glass, such as the handle of a jug, or the stem of a wine glass, can be added while the glass is still very hot, soft and sticky.

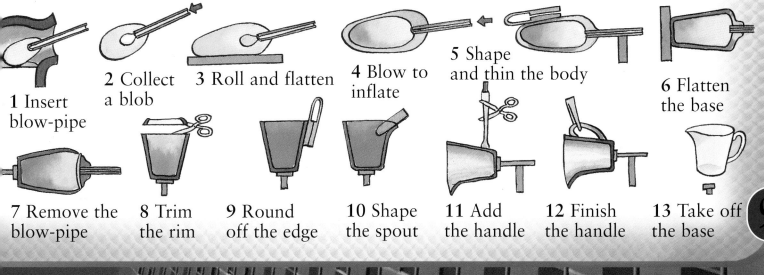

1 Insert blow-pipe

2 Collect a blob

3 Roll and flatten

4 Blow to inflate

5 Shape and thin the body

6 Flatten the base

7 Remove the blow-pipe

8 Trim the rim

9 Round off the edge

10 Shape the spout

11 Add the handle

12 Finish the handle

13 Take off the base

When oil floats on water, it spreads out into a thin, perfectly flat layer. Sheets of glass are now made in a similar way.

CROWNS AND CYLINDERS

Sheets of glass were once made in two ways. In the crown method, a blob of glass was spun around so it flattened into a wide disc. In the cylinder method, a glass blob was blown into a large cylinder, which was cut and flattened.

Glass panels covering whole skyscrapers are so smooth, they gleam like mirrors.

FLOAT GLASS

1 Raw materials: silica, lime, soda ash, cullet, and extra minerals rich in calcium, magnesium and aluminium

Raw materials melt in the furnace.

Workers check the process.

2 Melting furnace

3 Glass floats on molten tin

4 Controlled cooling

1,500°C   1,100°C Molten tin 600°C   550°C   200°C

Raw materials for float glass include cullet, which is scrap glass – old, broken and recycled bits and pieces. These are heated to 1,500°C to form a runny, molten mass.

The molten glass spreads over the perfectly smooth surface of molten tin, in a special air-proof chamber. Then the moving layer of glass is cooled slowly in another chamber.

A NEW INVENTION

In the 1950s, Pilkington glass-makers invented a faster way of making sheet glass. Compared to the old methods, the sheets were smoother, thinner, more even in thickness – and much larger. In this float glass process, raw ingredients are heated in the usual way, to make molten glass. This spreads out like treacle over the surface of a metal, tin, which is also heated so much that it is molten. We look through the results every day, as we gaze out of windows.

Careful cooling prevents cracks.

Sheets stored in the warehouse, before delivery.

5 Ribbon is cut into sheets

6 Stacking

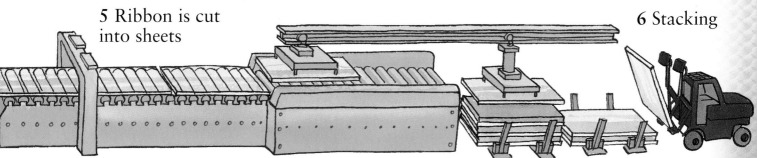

The glass emerges from the cooling chamber, or annealing lehr, as a clear, hard ribbon, without cracks or hazy areas. The ribbon is sliced by sharp blades into separate sheets.

The glass sheets are picked up by arms fitted with suction cups, and taken to warehouses. The float glass process carries on without a pause, for every minute of every day.

Hand-made glass items are beautiful but costly. Most glass objects, such as bottles, jars and light bulbs, are mass-produced by factory machines.

BLOBS AND GOBS

The machine measures out a gob – a blob of molten, runny glass. This flops into a hollow shape called the mould. The hole of the mould may be the shape of the final item, such as a rod or ball. The molten glass flows into it, takes up this shape, and goes cool and hard. The mould is then undone to release the item.

HOLLOW SHAPES

For hollow glass objects like bottles, the machine puffs a measured amount of air into the glass gob. This blows up and presses against the sides of the mould. In some cases the object is fully shaped in one mould. In other cases it is part-shaped first, in a blank mould. The resulting piece, the blank, is then put into a second mould, called the blow mould, for final shaping.

To make coloured lights, pigments (coloured substances) are mixed into the molten glass as it is made in the furnace.

STORY OF A BOTTLE

Molten glass from the furnace (shown below) flows straight into the bottle-making machine (shown in detail at the bottom). First the runny glass gob is part-blown into a bottle-like shape, called the blank, by a measured, pumped-in burst of air.

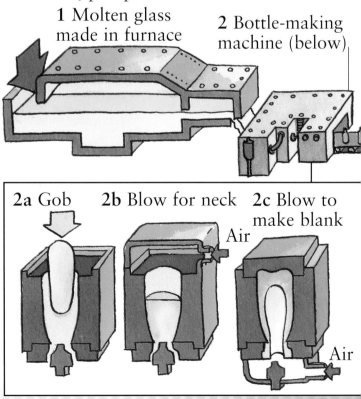

1 Molten glass made in furnace

2 Bottle-making machine (below)

2a Gob   2b Blow for neck   2c Blow to make blank
Air
Air

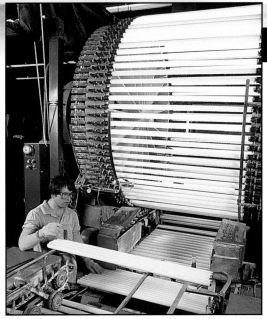

Manufacture of fluorescent glass tubes.

TUBES AND PIPES

Glass tubes are made for many purposes, such as strip (fluorescent) lights. As usual, the starting material is molten glass. It flows through the small gap around a spinning, tapered, hollow mandrel, as air blows through the mandrel. The result is a tube of soft, flexible glass, which is pulled along by the grips of a tractor-conveyor.

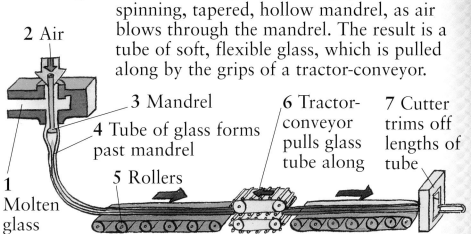

2 Air

3 Mandrel

4 Tube of glass forms past mandrel

6 Tractor-conveyor pulls glass tube along

7 Cutter trims off lengths of tube

5 Rollers

1 Molten glass

The blank is taken from the blank mould to the blow mould. More air is forced in to produce the final shape. The annealing lehr carefully controls the temperature of the bottles as they cool, so the glass stays strong.

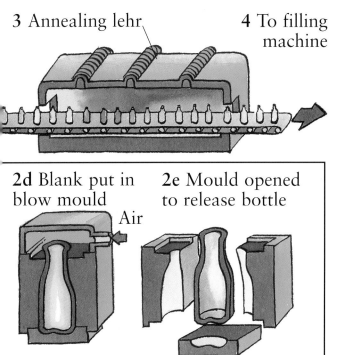

3 Annealing lehr

4 To filling machine

2d Blank put in blow mould

Air

2e Mould opened to release bottle

Bottle-making machines produce millions of bottles weekly. The bottle's shape comes directly from the blow mould. Some designs are known all over the world.

Glass windows and jars are useful and practical. But many glass objects are specially made *not* to be used. They are valued for their beauty, shape, colour and sparkle. They are known as decorative glass.

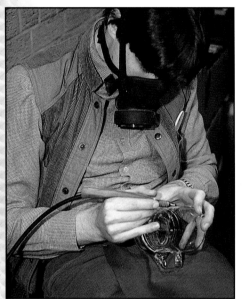 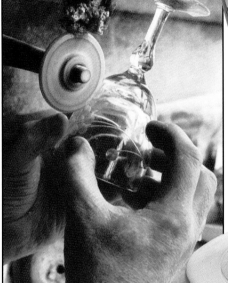

Glass's surface is rubbed away, or engraved, using tiny drills and grinding wheels. This very skilled job produces delicate patterns, like the wine glass, above.

NOT SHINY

Glass is not always shiny. Its smooth surface can be cut or roughened by various methods, to leave frosty-looking lines and patterns. The methods include engraving with rubbing and grinding tools, etching with chemicals such as acids, and sandblasting with high-power bursts of air carrying tiny particles. Glass can also be printed with inks, but these tend to rub away.

Glass is hard, but it can be marked by fast-moving particles such as sand. They remove the smooth shine and make the glass 'frosty' and opaque (no longer see-through).

First, the pattern is carefully designed and cut out of a sheet of tough plastic, the mask. This is stuck to the glass. Sand blasts the uncovered areas to make them opaque.

1 Thick plastic mask is made, with design cut out

2 Mask is stuck on to glass

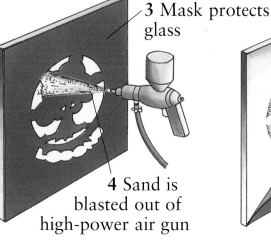

3 Mask protects glass

4 Sand is blasted out of high-power air gun

5 Mask is removed to reveal 'frosty' pattern

Patterned glass is decorative and lets in light. But it prevents a clear view, and so keeps a room private.

COLOURED GLASS

The colour of glass can be changed by painting it or covering it with plastic. But this only affects the surface. The glass itself can be coloured all the way through as it is made (see page 12), yet still remain see-through, by mixing in substances called pigments. Most pigments are based on metal-containing minerals. For example, copper-containing pigments produce red or light-blue glass. Chrome pigments make glass green, and cobalt gives glass a deep blue hue.

Facts from the **PAST**

The skill of glass-making combines art, craft and science. It thrived in Europe from the 12th century. From the 15th century, the major centre for decorative glass was Venice, in Italy.

16th-century glass-making.

15

Mass production by machines is ideal for everyday glass objects. But special hand-crafting skills are needed to create beautiful works of art in glass.

HOTTER AND HOTTER

Heat a piece of glass and it softens, so you can bend it. More heat makes it softer still, so you can squeeze it like modelling clay. Yet more heat makes glass molten and runny, like syrup. Different amounts of heat are the basis of shaping glass by hand.

These amazing glass 'clouds' in the hall of DG Bank, Berlin, are among the world's largest all-glass objects. They took months to make.

GLASS ZOO

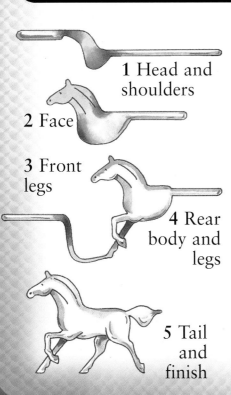

1 Head and shoulders

2 Face

3 Front legs

4 Rear body and legs

5 Tail and finish

Complicated, delicate items are made from separate pieces of glass. A length of rod is heated in the middle so that it sags into a blob. While still hot and soft, it is shaped with tweezers and pressing tools to form the features of the face. A thinner rod is heated so that it melts or welds on to the body. Then it is bent to make the leg. Piece by piece, a glass horse 'comes alive'. Or a fish, or a …

Special equipment for the science laboratory, like this flask with its many tubes, is 'custom made' by hand.

TRICKS OF THE TRADE

Traditional methods of hand-shaping glass, called lamp-working, have changed little for years. Two pieces of glass which are heated until just liquid will melt or fuse together. The two become one at an invisible join. A heated rod or tube can be stretched out very thin, which is called drawing, or squashed much thicker. Air blown into the hollow part of the object makes it balloon out like a bubble. Dimples or points are made with small spatulas, tweezers and other tools.

Hand-made perfume bottles from the 1930s show a style of design popular then – art deco.

Microwave melt?

Ideas for the FUTURE

Glass goes soft for shaping when it is very hot, usually more than 1,000°C. The heat usually comes from a lamp flame. One day, a new microwave oven could do the job. Glass for recycling could be microwave-melted in huge amounts, quickly and cheaply.

PRESSED GLASS

Pressing is a fairly simple method of making glass items such as cups and bowls, where the open end or mouth is the widest part. The gob (blob) of glass is pressed like a sandwich between the two parts of a mould. The surface design can be very complicated.

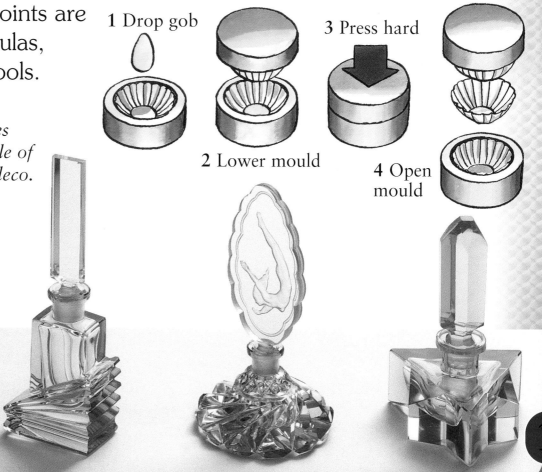

1 Drop gob

2 Lower mould

3 Press hard

4 Open mould

There is not just one kind of glass. There are thousands. Each has its own important features and special uses.

'COOKING' GLASS

Making different kinds of glass is like cooking. It depends on the mixture of ingredients or raw materials heated in the furnace. Adding a certain substance to the mixture can give the glass different features. For example, adding lead oxide, instead of calcium minerals, makes the glass glint, sparkle and twinkle in the light. This is called lead crystal glass. It is used especially for engraved or 'cut' wine glasses.

More special types of glass are shown here and on later pages.

Only a very few chemicals, such as hydrofluoric acid, can destroy glass. So glass flasks, jars and beakers are ideal for holding dangerous substances.

Tinted glass is used for sun-specs or 'shades'. Some types, called reactive sunglasses, only darken or tint when the sun comes out.

HOT OR COLD DRINK?

A vacuum flask has many ways of insulating, or slowing the flow of heat between outside and inside. The plastic case and the air gap inside it are good insulators. So is the glass of the inner container. This has two layers, and between them is nothing – a vacuum, another excellent insulator. The glass also has silvery coatings to reflect heat. The result is that hot drinks stay hot – or cold drinks keep cold.

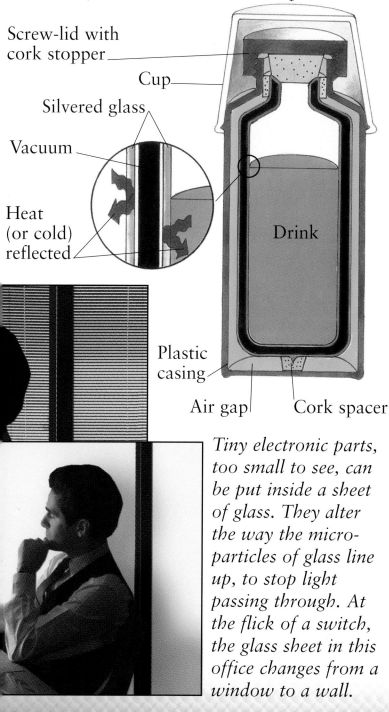

Screw-lid with cork stopper

Cup

Silvered glass

Vacuum

Heat (or cold) reflected

Drink

Plastic casing

Air gap

Cork spacer

Tiny electronic parts, too small to see, can be put inside a sheet of glass. They alter the way the micro-particles of glass line up, to stop light passing through. At the flick of a switch, the glass sheet in this office changes from a window to a wall.

MIRROR GLASS

Glass's shiny, smooth surface throws back or reflects some light, like a mirror. A real mirror has a glass front with a layer of very flat, shiny metallic substance behind it, to reflect nearly all the light. Shiny glass or a mirror is also very good at reflecting heat. In addition, glass is a thermal insulator – it prevents the flow of heat. So glass is excellent at keeping warmth in (or out).

Facts from the **PAST**

Clear glass lets sunshine through, bright and warm. But churches are usually meant to be cool and dim. So people made church windows of tinted or stained glass. Later, these became decorated with pictures.

A religious scene on stained glass.

19

Slivers of broken glass can be sharp and dangerous. Glass can be made safer, and less likely to shatter, when it is specially treated and manufactured.

POP! Most types of ordinary glass, like this light bulb, crack and shatter into small, sharp pieces when they are hit.

STRONG GLASS

A sudden knock or hit is called an impact. Many plastics are impact-resistant. They bend when hit, and do not shatter. Plastic is made of tiny but very long molecules, which make it flexible. Ordinary glass has no special tiny shapes or structures inside (see page 6). It is stiff and brittle. If hit, it does not bend, it breaks. It splits and shatters into sharp splinters. However, glass can be made stronger, tougher, and more impact-resistant, as shown here.

Toughened, impact-resistant glass laminates are used for high-speed vehicles such as cars, trains, planes and powerboats.

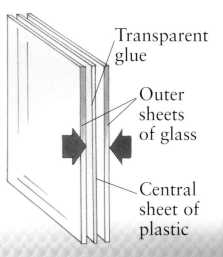

GLASS AND PLASTIC

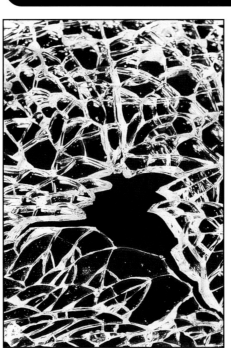

Close-up of a car's laminated windscreen, which has cracked, not shattered.

Laminated glass is like a 'sandwich'. Sheets of glass are stuck, by see-through glue, to a layer of clear plastic. This gives extra bending strength. If the glass should crack, the glue and plastic stop the pieces flying apart.

Transparent glue

Outer sheets of glass

Central sheet of plastic

Thermal toughening is different from the normal careful cooling, or annealing, of ordinary glass. Here, a large laboratory flask is thermally toughened with a special blowtorch.

Ideas for the FUTURE

Glass is clear and very hard, but not bendy. Plastics like acrylic are clear and bendy, but not very hard. Perhaps a new invention will be 'Flexiglass', which can bend. Then glass windows, covers and domes could be folded and put away!

Unfolding a glass window.

GLASS PLUS

Various layers can be added to glass, such as clear plastic sheet, plastic net or metal mesh. Dipping glass in powerful chemicals such as molten potassium salt also makes it stronger. Another method, thermal toughening, is shown on the next page.

GLASS AND WIRE MESH

Long, ribbon-like sheets of glass are heated until soft and bendy. One sheet is fed through rollers, and strong wire mesh is pressed on to it. Then another sheet of soft glass is pressed on top, to make one sheet of glass with the mesh inside. The glass cools hard and is trimmed into sheets. This type of glass is often used for protection and security. Even if the glass cracks, the wire mesh holds the pieces. The mesh also bends to take the impact, but does not break to leave a hole.

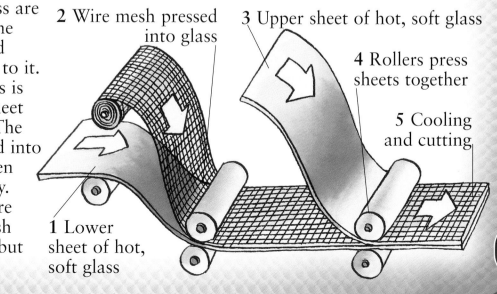

2 Wire mesh pressed into glass

3 Upper sheet of hot, soft glass

4 Rollers press sheets together

5 Cooling and cutting

1 Lower sheet of hot, soft glass

Ordinary glass begins to go soft when heated to about 700°C. But some glass can stand up to much higher temperatures, like flames, fires and furnaces.

BORO-GLASS

Heat-resistant glass, like ordinary glass, is mainly silica (SiO_2). But about one-tenth of it is the chemical boric oxide (B_2O_3). It's also called borosilicate glass.

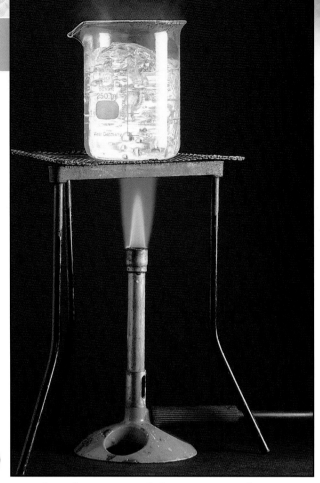

In the chemistry laboratory, glass beakers and flasks must be able to stand the heat of roaring flames.

TOUGHENED GLASS

Glass can be strengthened by heating it again, then cooling its surfaces very quickly with jets of cold air. The result is a 'sandwich', with two layers of fast-cooled glass on the outside, and a slow-cooled layer between them. You cannot see the layers since they are all transparent. This method is called thermal toughening. It works best with simple shapes like flat or curved sheets, bowls and wide-mouthed tumblers.

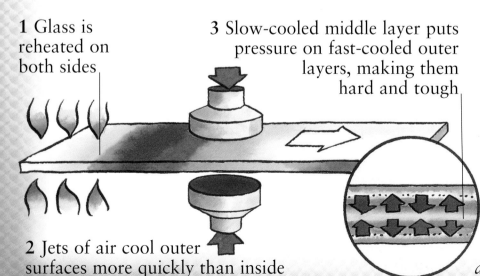

1 Glass is reheated on both sides

3 Slow-cooled middle layer puts pressure on fast-cooled outer layers, making them hard and tough

2 Jets of air cool outer surfaces more quickly than inside

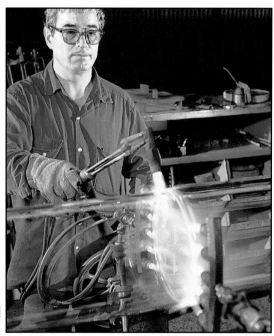

Chemistry glassware is shaped and finished before it is toughened.

Very bright lights get very hot. So heat-resistant glass is used for floodlights in stadiums and theatres, and for extra-bright vehicle headlamps.

HEAT AND LIGHT

Borosilicate glass does not start to go soft until it is hotter than 800°C. And it does not melt until 1,300°C or above. This makes it very useful where temperatures are high – not only near furnaces and flames, but also for cookers and ovens. 'Oven-proof' and 'flame-proof' glass dishes, bowls and saucepans are usually made from this type of glass. Another important use is for very bright, high-power lights. But borosilicate glass is more costly than ordinary glass. Its raw materials are more expensive, and they must be heated to greater temperatures in the furnace when the glass is made.

PYREX
PERMET DE SURVEILLER
A TOUT INSTANT LA CUISSON
PARCEQU'IL EST
TRANSPARENT

See what's cooking!

Facts from the **PAST**

The first main heat-resistant glass was invented in 1915 by the Corning Glass Works. It was given the trade name of Pyrex. Gradually it was used to make cooking bowls and dishes. Their great advantage, compared to metal or pottery, was that you could see if the contents were burning, without taking off the lid!

23

Most glass is stiff. If you try to bend it, it snaps. But you could tie glass fibres into knots!

'HAIRS' OF GLASS

If glass is made in the form of long, narrow rods, or fibres, then it is more flexible or bendy. Glass fibres may be thinner than human hairs. They can be produced as separate strands, or matted together as wool.

GLASS WOOL

1 Molten glass

Like most glass-making methods, glass wool begins with molten (melted) glass. This flows into a spinning dish called a crown, with hundreds of tiny holes around its edge. The glass spurts out of the holes and quickly hardens into fibres.

As glass strands are thrown out of the spinning crown, blasts of hot air make them even longer and thinner.

A bonding chemical is heated to stick the fibres together, into a loose mat or blanket. This is trimmed along the edges and cut into lengths.

3 Bonding chemical added

4 Chemical sets in oven

8 Rolled-up lengths of glass wool matting

5 Roller

6 Trimmer

7 Cutter

2 Fast-spinning 'crown' throws out thin strands of glass through tiny holes

KEEP THE HEAT

A major use for glass fibres is insulation, to keep heat in (or out). Glass itself is a good insulator. A layer or blanket of glass fibres traps lots of air, and trapped air is also a good insulator. And glass fibres last for a very long time. Unlike natural fibres such as wool or cotton, glass does not rot away or go mouldy if it gets damp.

GLASS AND PLASTIC

Glass fibres are also put into GRP, glass-reinforced plastic. The fibres give strength and stiffness, while the plastic bends to cope with knocks. GRP is impact-resistant and can be moulded into shapes such as 'hard-hat' helmets, boat hulls and car bodies.

Glass wool is ideal for insulation in roofs, walls and floors. It keeps heat in and cold out, does not rot or catch fire, and also lessens outside noises.

GLASS STRANDS

Very long, hair-like fibres of glass are formed by pulling molten glass through tiny holes in metal shapes called bushes. The fibres come together into bundles called strands, which are like thin 'ropes' of glass. These are used to strengthen or reinforce plastic and even cement.

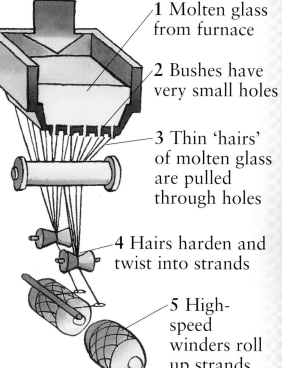

1 Molten glass from furnace

2 Bushes have very small holes

3 Thin 'hairs' of molten glass are pulled through holes

4 Hairs harden and twist into strands

5 High-speed winders roll up strands

Ideas for the FUTURE

Warm 'thermal' clothing is made of fibres, woven or matted into layers. One day, glass fibres may be used. Of course, they would have to be safe to wear, without harming the skin. They could work like glass in a greenhouse, to reflect and keep in the body's heat. They would also be strong, waterproof, rotproof and long-lasting.

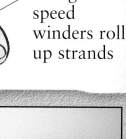

Glass fibre clothing would be ideal for mountaineers.

25

Optical glass is specially made to be very clear indeed. It is used in spectacles, telescopes, cameras and fibre-optic cables.

SEE THE LIGHT

The scientific study of light is called *optics*. One of its main areas is the study of how glass bounces or reflects light, bends or refracts it, and splits it into different colours.

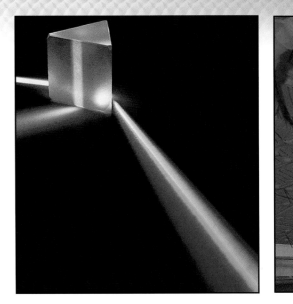

Ordinary 'white' light, from the Sun, is really a mixture of all the colours of the rainbow. A triangle-shaped glass block, called a prism, bends the colours by different amounts and so separates them.

Optical fibres are grouped into bundles called cables.

OPTICAL FIBRES

Each optical fibre is thinner than a human hair. It consists of a long, flexible rod made of two types of special glass, one inside the other. The fibre is formed by pulling molten glass through two tiny holes (opposite). Flashes of light pass along the inner layer, or core. When they reach the different glass of the outer layer, or cladding, they reflect back. In this way the flashes zig-zag along the core, carrying information.

Light zig-zags along core of optical fibre

CRYSTAL CLEAR

Optical glass is used to make curved lenses, angular prisms, mirrors and other shapes that alter light. It must be very clear, so that it lets light pass through perfectly, without changing or distorting the light rays in unwanted ways.

Some of the largest glass items are lenses and mirrors made for giant telescopes. This special furnace heats glass until it just melts, then spins it around, so the glass spreads to form a curved mirror.

FLASHING FIBRES

Optical fibres carry flashes of laser light which are codes for messages, such as telephone calls, 'cable' TV programmes or computer information. The fibres work faster, and carry more signals, than electrical signals passing along metal wires.

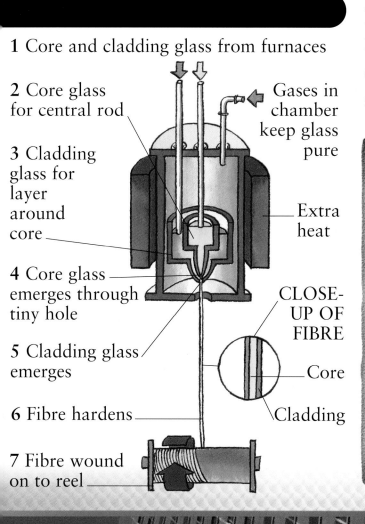

1 Core and cladding glass from furnaces

2 Core glass for central rod

3 Cladding glass for layer around core

4 Core glass emerges through tiny hole

5 Cladding glass emerges

6 Fibre hardens

7 Fibre wound on to reel

Gases in chamber keep glass pure

Extra heat

CLOSE-UP OF FIBRE

Core

Cladding

Facts from the **PAST**

In the 1600s, before very clear optical glass was invented, people made the first telescopes and microscopes from 'natural glass'. This has formed in the rocks over a very long time, by natural processes. It consists of large, clear crystals of quartzite and similar minerals.

Quartz crystal

Glass is made mainly from silica – sand. On the beach, or in a desert, supplies of sand may seem endless. So can we go on throwing away old glass, and making new glass, for ever?

USE AGAIN

The raw materials for making glass include many other minerals and chemicals, and some of these are very costly. Also the glass-making furnaces and other equipment use huge amounts of energy, especially heat. This is why it is very important to re-use glass items like bottles and jars, rather than buying new ones.

Recycling uses one-third less energy than making new glass, and it cuts down on raw materials by three-quarters. 'Bottle banks' keep the colours separate – clear, brown and green.

One of the first great glass buildings was the Crystal Palace, London, England. It was finished in 1851. Intended to last for centuries, it was destroyed by fire in 1936.

Even in the hi-tech glass industry of the future, skill and craftsmanship will still be needed to shape specialist glassware, as seen above.

RECYCLING GLASS

Glass is one of the easiest substances to recycle. Old, broken and scrap glass, known as cullet, is cleaned and crushed, then added to the furnace at the start of the process. Nearly all neighbourhoods have glass recycling containers.

INVENTING NEW GLASS

For centuries, people have invented new kinds of glass, and new uses for it. This is certain to continue. Glass that is stronger than steel, windows that change colour or show pictures – glass will continue to be one of the world's most useful materials.

Ideas for the **FUTURE**

TV specs or visors can show programmes on tiny screens. New kinds of glass would make the pictures sharper, brighter and more colourful. Add a tiny computer, and a voice-controller, and you could surf the Internet too!

The Internet – in your face!

29

GLASS PRODUCT	QUALITIES AND METHOD OF MANUFACTURE
Soda-lime silica glass ('ordinary' glass)	Inexpensive, quite strong, easy to shape and also to clean and recycle; used for bottles, jars and everyday containers
Soda-lime silica glass with extra sodium	Relatively inexpensive, made by float process, resists weather, can be toughened; used for window panes and similar sheets
Soda-lime silica glass with even more sodium	Fairly inexpensive, can be blown or shaped quickly from ribbons, clear, resists changes in temperature; used for light bulbs and electric lamps, fluorescent light tubes, vacuum flasks
Soda-lime silica glass with extra magnesium and aluminium	Relatively inexpensive, tough, can withstand regular use, bright and clear, does not affect foods or drinks; used for tumblers, bowls, dishes, plates and everyday glassware
Soda-lime silica glass with extra minerals	Resists weather and temperature, easily pressed, strong; used for glass building blocks, walls, stairs, floors, roofs, partitions
Soda-lime silica glass with extra calcium and aluminium	Strong but light, resists chemicals and also damp, heat and electricity, can be spun or drawn into very thin strands; used for glass fibres and wool, glass-reinforced plastic
Borosilicate glass (such as Pyrex)	Resists chemicals, heat, microwaves, strong, easy to clean; used for test-tubes and laboratory equipment, ovenproof cookware
Lead glass (up to one-third lead oxide)	Heavy or dense, can be shaped with great precision, brilliant sparkling finish, can be engraved and patterned; used for 'lead crystal' wine glasses and containers, hand-made glass ornaments, decorations and works of art
Lead glass – with added lead (up to two-thirds lead oxide)	Extremely heavy or dense, stops dangerous rays; used as shielding for protection against radioactivity in nuclear power stations, atomic research laboratories
Optical glass (varies greatly in raw materials)	Extremely clear, can be polished, resists temperature changes; used for cameras, telescopes, microscopes, binoculars, lasers, spectacles and other devices which work using light
Laminate glass (as a sandwich with plastic)	Very hard, strong, shatterproof; used for windscreens, safety screens and similar see-through protection from impacts

GLOSSARY

amorphous
'Shapeless', with no particular shape or structure.

anneal
To strengthen or toughen a substance by a combination of very careful heating and cooling. The special oven-cooler used for this process is called an annealing lehr.

cullet
Glass which is old, broken, rejected, scrapped or recycled, and used again in glass-making.

draw
In glass-shaping, to pull or stretch soft or molten glass, so that it becomes longer and thinner.

impact
A knock, hit, bump or similar physical shock.

molten
A substance which is so hot, it has melted into a liquid, which can ooze and flow.

parison
A partly-shaped lump of glass, which will be fully shaped by blowing or moulding to form the finished object.

pigment
A substance used to give colour to glass, paints, inks, cloth and similar materials.

reflect
To bounce back, as when sound waves bounce off a wall as an echo, or light rays reflect off a mirror to form an image.

refract
To bend or change direction, as when light rays bend as they pass into or out of a glass object.

silica
A substance made of the chemicals silicon and oxygen, as silicon dioxide (SiO_2). It makes up the mineral quartz, which is familiar as sand, and is the main raw material for making glass.